GANDHI

A Discussion on the Struggle for Human Rights

Conversations between Daisaku Ikeda,
President of Soka Gakkai International and
representatives of the Soka Gakkai
youth division of Japan.

Soka Gakkai Malaysia

Contents

PROFILE

Daisaku Ikeda was born in Tokyo on January 2, 1928, the fifth of eight children, to a family of seaweed farmers. As a teenager he lived through the devastation of World War II, and its senseless horror left an indelible mark on his life. His four older brothers were drafted into military service; the eldest was killed in action. These experiences, along with the human anguish and turmoil he witnessed in the years following the war, continue to fuel his lifelong quest to root out the fundamental causes of human conflict and suffering.

In 1947, at the age of nineteen, he met Mr Josei Toda (1900-1958), 2nd president of Soka Gakkai. Soka Gakkai is a lay Buddhist society which activities are based on the philosophy of the 13th-century Buddhist teacher and reformer, Nichiren. Mr Ikeda found in Josei Toda a completely open and unaffected man, a person of unshakeable conviction with a unique gift for explaining profound Buddhist concepts in logical, accessible terms. Mr Ikeda, who is an avid reader of poetry, literature and philosophy in his youth, displays an insatiable thirst for knowledge. Amidst poverty and ill health, he continued his studies under the tutelage of educator and publisher, Mr Toda, whom he regarded as his lifelong mentor.

Through his relationship with Josei Toda, Mr Ikeda came to understand and respect the Soka Gakkai's philosophy as a concrete means to realise the universal value of human dignity and peace. Mr Toda, together with Soka Gakkai founder and 1st president Tsunesaburo Makiguchi (1871-1944), had been jailed in 1943 for refusing to compromise their religious beliefs in support of the Japanese war effort. Mr Makiguchi died in prison at the age of seventy-three. Mr Toda emerged from the ordeal of imprisonment just prior to Japan's surrender, and dedicated the remainder of his life to the reconstruction and development of Soka Gakkai.

In 1952, Mr Ikeda married Kaneko Shiraki. Comrade and confidante ever since, she has been his constant companion in his journey for peace for more than forty years after Mr Toda's death. Mr Ikeda succeeded him as president of the Soka Gakkai. Under his leadership, the movement began an era of innovation and expansion, becoming actively engaged in cultural and educational endeavours worldwide. In 1975, Mr Ikeda became the president of Soka Gakkai International (SGI), an association that today includes more than fourteen million members worldwide, with lay organisations in 186 countries and territories.

People's Hearts and Society:

The Arena of Gandhi's Endeavours

Gandhi was of the opinion that the purpose of religion is to serve those who live amid reality. That is why he felt that a religion which is not involved in actual society does not deserve to be called a religion. Gandhi's religious practice was to struggle for the rights and happiness of the people. "Get close to the people," and "Go among the people," were his mottoes, the very essence of his spirit.

Youth Representative

President Ikeda, you started practising Nichiren Daishonin's Buddhism in August 1947 during the exact, same month India gained its independence. At the very time when Mahatma Gandhi's struggle for human rights had turned the impossible into the possible by achieving India's independence, you took the first step in your own fight for human rights. A member of one SGI youth cultural exchange delegation to India remarked that this appears to be a mysterious succession of events.

SGI President Ikeda met Soka Gakkai 2nd president Josei Toda on August 14, 1947, and started practising Nichiren Daishonin's Buddhism on August 24. India's independence was achieved on August 15, 1947.

President Ikeda

Quite aside from whether there is a mystic connection between these two events or not, back in those days I watched the developments unfolding in India with great interest.

Not even those who participated in the Indian independence movement themselves thought that independence would be achieved during their lifetime. However, Gandhi's selflessness liberated the great power of the people and changed the course of history. He achieved what may be called a miracle.

Gandhi removed the chains of subordination that had bound the hearts of the Indian people for several centuries. He also succeeded in making the British oppressors realise their disgraceful conduct, fundamentally changing Indo-British relations.

Gandhi's struggle, more than anything, was aimed at changing people's hearts and minds. For this reason, he lived out his entire life persistently striving to change himself first.

The front on which he pursued his endeavours was the hearts of human beings.

Centennial of Gandhi's Visit to South Africa

Youth Representative
Gandhi's religious conviction gave birth to an immense political force that has rarely been found elsewhere in modern times. Was Gandhi a religious figure, a political leader, or both?

President Ikeda
This year (1993) marks the 100th anniversary of Gandhi's arrival in South Africa (in 1893, at the age of twenty-three). For a total of twenty-two years, he fought against discrimination there. His experience in South Africa formed the foundation and the departure for the subsequent Indian nationalist movement. For it was there that he had firmly grasped the way to carry out a human rights movement.

During his stay in South Africa, Gandhi asserted that although his critics called him 'a saint who is lost in the field of politics,' he was, in fact, a political leader striving with all his energies to become a saint.

Gandhi and his wife Kasturba (centre) with fellow settlers at the Phoenix Settlement. (Natal, South Africa, 1904-1914.)

A True Religion Involves Itself in Society and People

Youth Representative
The label, 'a saint who is lost in the field of politics', would seem to contain the criticism that religious believers should stay and meditate in caves or temples.

President Ikeda
Yes. But, Gandhi was of the opinion that the purpose of religion is to serve those who live amid reality. That is why he felt that a religion which is not involved in actual society does not deserve to be called a religion.

Gandhi's religious practice was to struggle for the rights and happiness of the people. "Get close to the people," and "Go among the people," were his mottoes, the very essence of his spirit.

Meanwhile, in the realm of activities concerned with improving people's lives, Gandhi disciplined himself through religion, and inspired others.

In his autobiography, Gandhi wrote: "To see the universal and all-pervading Spirit of Truth face to face one must be able to love the meanest of creation as oneself. And a man who aspires after that cannot afford to keep out of any field of life. That is why my devotion to Truth has drawn me into the field of politics; and I can say without the slightest hesitation, and yet in all humility, that those who say that religion has nothing to do with politics do not know what religion means."[1]

Youth Representative

Because Gandhi was a religious and spiritual person, he was active in society. At the same time, however, his societal activities remained religiously and spiritually pure.

President Ikeda

The arena in which Gandhi carried out his activities was not in a temple but in actual society; it was not in a secluded mountain but among the people.

President Toda once said, "Youth, be patriots!" He also

---

1. Mohandas K. Gandhi, *An Autobiography: The Story of My Experiments with Truth* (Boston: Beacon Press, 1962), pg 504.

warned, "We must not become religious professionals!"

Mr Toda was born (in 1900) during the Meiji era. Although the word 'patriot' may have an old-fashioned ring to it, it refers to a person who is determined to stand up and save people from unhappiness. The person who is completely devoted to working for humanity, not just in the realm of politics but in every sphere of life, is a true practitioner of Buddhism. This is the practice of securing the peace of the land through the propagation of true Buddhism.

The Youth Carried on the Struggle

Youth Representative

Many youth carried on the movement begun by Gandhi. Among these people are New Delhi's Gandhi Memorial Hall (Gandhi Smriti and Darshan Samiti) Vice-Chairperson B.N. Pande and the late J.P. Narayan, both of whom you have met.

President Ikeda

Another successor of Gandhi's legacy is Usha Mehta, the current president of Bombay's Gandhi Memorial Hall (Mani Bhavan Gandhi Sangrahalaya). Dr Mehta, together with the centre's general director, Madame Usha Gokani, Gandhi's granddaughter, welcomed the SGI youth exchange delegation to India. They also presented me with a copy of the autobiography and some photographs of the Indian human rights leader.

Gandhi with textile workers at Lancashire, UK. The textile workers became unemployed due to his protest against foreign cloth in India. Yet, the workers cheered him on. One of them said, "I am one of the unemployed, but if I was in India, I would say the same thing that Mr Gandhi is saying."
(September 1931)

Dr Mehta is a veteran of many struggles, dating back to when she was a young child. Vice-General Director Akash K. Ouchi of the Bharat Soka Gakkai, the SGI organisation in India, has heard her experiences first-hand and told me about them.

Youth Representative
Has Dr Mehta lived in Bombay all her life?

President Ikeda
I believe she moved there at the age of thirteen (in 1933)

8

because her father, who was a judge, was transferred to the Indian city. She once said that in those days the whole city was afire with the resistance movement against colonial rule and the campaign to obtain freedom. Gandhi's non-violent movement had captured the hearts and minds of the entire country.

In any endeavour, it is vital to win the hearts of the people.

Not only men and women but also children participated in the nationalist movement. It is said that the children formed peace corps on their own. The boys called themselves the 'monkey corps'. When the police came around, they all shrieked like monkeys. And because there were so many of them shrieking, the police would run away.

The girls formed a group which they called the cat corps. At the sight of the police, everyone would meow like cats. Confronted by a multitude of girls meowing at them, the police were at an absolute loss as to what to do.

You can tell from these activities of the youth that this was a movement truly created by the people, can't you?

Youthful Demonstrators Attacked

President Ikeda

On one occasion, the cat corps organised a march in which they paraded the Indian national flag — an activity that was prohibited at that time. But the youth were daring. The march was obstructed by the police who violently beat the demonstrators and the girl who was carrying the flag was knocked out cold.

9

Dr Usha Mehta.

The authorities were cruel to cast an evil spell over human being.

However, Dr Mehta and the other leaders of the cat corps were not afraid of the police. They racked their brains over a way to continue their march, even should the police appear on the scene to stop them. That day, the members of the cat corps came up with the idea of making clothes out of the Indian flag which they could wear in the march. Some members of the Indian National Congress supplied them with the necessary material, and they all set to work on sewing the garments.

The members worked all night long until their family members finally started to worry and came looking for them. It is said that when the family members learnt what the young people were doing, they joined in, staying up all night to help finish making the clothes.

The next day, the girls put on the clothes they had fashioned out of the flags and resumed their marching. The police must have been completely dumbfounded. It was unthinkable that they should raise their hand against the national flag. In the end, the police stood by helplessly, while the march finished in a great success.

A victory had been won by the courage and wisdom of the youth.

Confronting Oppression with the Power of Truth

Lies make people weak. To live a life based on the truth makes people strong. Those who are two-faced or hypocritical become weak at the crucial moment. Those whose hearts are free of lies and falsehood are strong. The underlying principle of Gandhi's human rights movement was satyagraha (devotion to truth), which sought to establish the power of truth as the prevailing force in people's hearts and lives.

Youth Representative

When did Dr Usha Mehta, the current president of Bombay's Gandhi Memorial Hall (Mani Bhavan Gandhi Sangrahalaya), first meet Mahatma Gandhi, her mentor in life?

President Ikeda

I have heard that they met when she was eight years old.

Her father was a judge in Kheda City in Gujarat State (the same state in which Gandhi was born). One day, the judge took his family to Gandhi's *ashram* (a colony for communal living established by Gandhi) in the suburbs of Ahmedabad in the same state.

They arrived that night just as Gandhi was about to go outside to do his evening prayers, and he asked the Mehta family to join him. Upon finishing their prayers, the young Mehta greeted Gandhi, expressing her deep respects.

Her father then asked Gandhi, "Would you please say a few words to my child that will be useful to her in life?"

Gandhi replied, "You mustn't say things that aren't true. Speak only the truth."

These words determined the rest of Dr Mehta's life. Even though she was only eight years old, he spoke to her as he would to an adult, saying, "Speak only the truth."

Lies make people weak. To live a life based on the truth makes people strong. Those who are two-faced or hypocritical become weak at a crucial moment. Those whose hearts are free of lies and falsehood are strong.

The underlying principle of Gandhi's human rights

movement was *satyagraha* (devotion to truth), which sought to establish the power of truth as the prevailing force in people's hearts and lives.

Gandhi held the view that as long as the power of the authorities is based on hate and violence, it could only be an animalistic power. Moreover, he believed that to fight against this problem by simply succumbing to one's own animalistic urge to use violence would provide no fundamental solution. Instead, he taught people to arm themselves with the lofty power of truth and humanity, telling them that, ultimately, there is no stronger weapon.

Gandhi's philosophy was criticised as being unrealistic. But, history was to prove just how effective it could be.

A Pledge to Fight for Independence

Youth Representative
The words, "Speak only the truth", which Gandhi spoke to the young Dr Mehta, were also deeply significant, weren't they?

President Ikeda
Because it was already quite late, Gandhi invited Mr Mehta and his family to stay the night at the ashram.

The next morning when they were saying their goodbyes, Gandhi asked Dr Mehta's father with genuine concern: "Could you lose your job as a judge for having stayed the night at an ashram?" For it was a matter of course that Gandhi and his followers were always closely watched by the authorities.

Dr Mehta's father answered, "To meet you, I would be happy to lose my job." He was a person of strong conviction.

Later, her father became the judge for the area where the ashram was located and the Mehta family was able to visit Gandhi quite frequently.

In 1929, India set its sights on achieving complete independence. And, on January 26, 1930, the Indian National Congress pledged itself to a declaration of independence. Thereafter, every year on that date [until independence was finally achieved in 1947], people turned out for mass demonstrations throughout the country, waving the tricolour national flag of India.

The people renewed their vow to oust the colonial authorities.

Youth Representative
Speaking of January 26, that is also the same day as SGI Day.

The SGI was inaugurated on January 26, 1975. On the same day, in 1950, India adopted a new constitution to establish the Republic of India, and the Indian people still celebrate the occasion today as Republic Day.

Rejection of a Vile Monopoly

President Ikeda
Shortly thereafter, the non-cooperation movement began, which was symbolised by the famous march to boycott the

15

On March 12, 1930, Gandhi along with 78 men and women, left Sabarmati Ashram on foot for Dandi Beach, 241 miles away. This historic march was to break the Salt Law passed by the British which deprived the poor man of his right to make his own salt.

monopoly on salt — the so-called 'Salt March' (in 1930).

Salt is an essential commodity in our daily lives. Especially in a country as hot as India, salt is of vital importance to the lives of those who toil under harsh conditions and live by the sweat of their labours. However, the British government held a monopoly on salt and levied a high tax on it. Poor people could not even buy a sufficient amount. And if someone was found to possess salt which they had acquired from outside of the monopoly, they were punished.

Gandhi openly challenged this. He reasoned that salt is a blessing from nature just like the air and water. Salt is something that can be easily obtained from seawater; it certainly

Mahatma Gandhi breaking the Salt Law by picking up a lump of natural salt at the Dandi Beach. Having walked for twenty-four days, 241 miles, in the early hours of April 6, Gandhi picked up a little lump of natural salt left by the waves on Dandhi Beach. This simple act was immediately followed by a nation wide non-violent defiance of the Salt Law. Thousands of men and women were arrested, including Gandhi.

is not an exclusive commodity for a privileged few. He declared the situation to be a 'vile monopoly'.

Gandhi and his followers then left the ashram, and began their march to the seashore at Dandi. Gandhi, who was sixty years old at the time, walked for twenty-four consecutive days. And with each passing day, the participants in the march increased.

When they reached the seashore, Gandhi gathered the solid salt that was scattered on the beach. This was a simple action. However, it was also a historic declaration that the Indian people would no longer tolerate this evil monopoly.

Gandhi's burning conviction that Indians could manage to run their country [without foreign interference] spread throughout the land. All over India, people started to manufacture their own salt *en masse*. Oppression and arrests continued.

Armed with the Power of the Human Spirit

President Ikeda

Dr Mehta has said of that time, "Even my grandmother made salt at my family's house in my hometown. We made salt based on the conviction that in doing so, we were fighting against the law that was imposed by the colonial rulers. In this way, the women stood up to reply to Gandhi's call.

"Gandhi practised non-violence in the arenas of society and politics. He called for the people to stand up and confront wild violence with the power of the human spirit, based on *satyagraha*. This became his strong appeal to the people, especially women."

She also commented, "I studied Marx and Lenin when I was in college, but there was nothing about non-violence in their teachings."

Youth Representative

Speaking of monopolies, the Nikken sect, based on its assertion that only priests have the right to conduct funeral and memorial services, has continued to intimidate believers with threats that they will fall into hell if they fail to obey its directives, and to engage in harassment that clearly infringes on the believers' human rights.

However, the people will no longer be deceived. The religious reformation that is being carried out by the SGI, including the conducting of funeral services by lay members, is having a great influence on the religious sphere as a whole, as well as in society.

The Folly of Trying to Own the Sun

President Ikeda

The Mystic Law is no one's exclusive possession. Just like the sun and water are no one's sole belongings.

Only one's faith can draw forth the power of the Mystic Law. And we, the members of the SGI, possess truly strong and correct faith.

From the perspective of Buddhism, the true greatness of the SGI is unfathomable. It's inexpressible. Comprehending its full significance is impossible. If you can absorb this fact, then everything you do in life will have meaning.

The people of India had stood up. Their call was "Let's create everything with our own hands!" And, it was Gandhi's spinning wheel that was the symbol of the rejection of foreign manufactured cloth and the struggle for independence.

The Desire to Liberate India from all Fetters

President Ikeda

Let me tell you about the time that Dr Mehta, together with her

Gandhi sitting before a *charkha*, the spinning wheel used by peasants all over India. He made it a point to spin every day, wherever he was. The charkha was his symbol of *Swadeshi* (indigenous) industry and the core of his philosophy of self-reliance.

older sister, went to ask if they could join one of the camps of the independence movement. Dr Mehta was eleven years old at the time.

Gandhi said to them: "You both are wearing foreign clothes, aren't you? I won't permit either of you to join if you don't wear hand-spun clothes." In other words, he was saying, "Haven't you done away with the evil customs of the past yet?"

The two sisters then went to their aunt's house to borrow some hand-spun clothes. The next day, they returned to request Gandhi's permission.

"Look, *Bapu* (The Indian word for father, which was a term of affection used to address Gandhi), we are wearing hand-spun clothes."

"That makes me happy. But I still can't grant the two of you permission to join. In order to participate in this movement, both of you must promise to wear hand-spun clothes for the rest of your lives."

"We promise."

"That's not all. Neither of you can ever get married."

At this, their aunt who was with them said, "Don't you think you're being a little too strict on them?"

Gandhi replied: "Well then, neither of you must marry anyone who demands a dowry. You should marry someone who will assist you in your activities to liberate the country."

The two promised to what Gandhi had asked and were permitted to participate in the independence movement.

Gandhi no doubt saw dowries as an evil custom that lowers marriage into nothing but a business transaction. He may have hoped that marriage in this new age would be a union between partners who aspire for the same goal and share a common ideal.

The Indian human rights leader constantly remarked that he was not interested only in liberating India from the yoke of colonial rule, but in emancipating India from all fetters that bound it.

Gandhi strove to sever the chains that confined the heart of every person he met, as this example of Dr Mehta portrays. He continued to carry out this painstaking task of offering personal guidance to one person after another.

Advancing with Total Commitment to One's Struggle

When Dr Mehta was a student at the University of Bombay (Wilson College), she said to the nationalist leader: "I also want to stay at the ashram and participate in the independence movement. Please allow me to do so."

However, Gandhi admonished her: "Now is the time for you to study. Go back to Bombay and study hard."

Most leaders would rejoice when the number of their active membership increases. However, truly humanistic leaders are constantly thinking about each person's future and setting their sights on the long-range goals of the movement they spearhead.

President Ikeda

A battle must not be fought half-heartedly. If you are going to fight, you must completely devote yourself to the struggle; otherwise you will be defeated.

Driving a car is the same way. If you are not serious, you will have an accident. Then, not only will you be miserable but you will bring trouble and grief upon others.

In mountain climbing, as well, it would be extremely dangerous for you to think lightly of the climb or to disrupt the unity of your team. You would not be able to reach the glorious summit. For a victorious ascent, everyone must summon forth all the wisdom and strength they possess.

Buddhism is win or lose, and since all phenomena are encompassed by the Buddhist Law, everything is a struggle between winning or losing — a clear-cut struggle in which there are only two outcomes: victory or defeat. Achieving ultimate victory in our lives is a process of concluding every challenge, each day, in victory. If each small battle is inconclusive, there can be no victory; and that means defeat.

Ultimately, whether we are victorious in our lives and throughout the three existences of past, present and future is determined by our efforts today; it is determined by our *ichinen*, or resolve, at this moment.

Now is the Time to Study

President Ikeda

Dr Usha Mehta, the current president of Bombay's Gandhi

Memorial Hall (Mani Bhavan Gandhi Sangrahalaya), also fought with great determination and dedication. After completing a master's degree at the University of Bombay, she launched herself heart and soul into the struggle for independence.

Youth Representative

Until she finished her degree, Dr Mehta gave first priority to her studies, didn't she?

President Ikeda

That is what Gandhi told her to do. When Dr Mehta was a student at the University of Bombay (Wilson College), she said to the nationalist leader: "I also want to stay at the ashram and participate in the independence movement. Please allow me to do so."

However, Gandhi admonished her: "Now is the time for you to study. Go back to Bombay and study hard."

Most leaders would rejoice when the number of their active membership increases. However, truly humanistic leaders are constantly thinking about each person's future and setting their sights on the long-range goals of the movement they spearhead.

Following her graduation from the University of Bombay, Dr Mehta continued on to law school. At that time, Gandhi asked her to help with the translation of the movement's organ newsletter. Because of this, she was able to participate in the independence movement while pursuing her studies.

Conveying the Mentor's Message
to All Humanity

President Ikeda

After completing her studies (in 1941), Dr Mehta gathered together with other university graduates to deliberate on how to proceed with the movement.

For quite some time, Gandhi's newspaper had been delivered to rural areas and his message spread in this way. But, there was a limit to the number of people it could reach. How could the students contribute to passing on their mentor's message to more people, to more remote rural villages?

India's population in those days was concentrated largely in rural areas. It was essential that the independence movement won over the hearts of the people. As a result of their discussions, the students decided to create a radio station. This, of course, would have to be carried out in top secret, hidden well away from the eyes of the government. World War II was also under way, adding further to the already tense social environment in India.

The youth sought out an engineer and asked him to build the equipment they would need to set up a radio station. The engineer supported their idea and agreed to cooperate. But, what was to be done about the expenses? The young people pooled together all of their savings, but it did not even amount to a quarter of what they needed.

As they were wondering what to do, Dr Mehta's aunt, who had been listening in the next room, gave the youth all her

26

precious jewellery, telling them to use it for their cause. The youth, filled with a deep sense of appreciation, endeavoured not to use the jewels unless they had to, managing somehow to raise the necessary funds and establish the radio station.

They set up a radio station specifically for the promotion of freedom and independence; it was the fruit of the youth's creative flexibility and their tireless challenging spirit.

Incidentally, in the 'Voice-Aid' campaign organised by the Soka Gakkai youth division [and conducted with the support of the United Nations Transitional Authority in Cambodia (UNTAC) from June through December 1992], both Soka Gakkai members and the Japanese public donated portable radios to [assist in the democratisation process in] Cambodia. The power of youth is truly magnificent.

The approximately 284,000 portable radios donated were used in publicising and promoting the Cambodian general elections held in May 1993.

Indian Youths' Efforts Gain Recognition

Youth Representative

What was the reaction to the student's radio station?

President Ikeda

It was extremely positive. When the broadcasts began, they drew delighted responses from throughout the country. The leader of the Indian National Congress [which had been

27

promoting the independence movement], Mr Rohini, sent a message to the youth responsible for the radio station, saying that he would like to meet them. They received a warm welcome at the leader's house. Dr Mehta says that even now she cannot forget the great honour she felt that day.

Young people must be treasured. There are far too many leaders whose attitude towards youth is patronising or exploitative.

Mr Rohini supported the youth, telling them that the Indian National Congress would give them full financial backing, and that they could therefore freely continue in their activities. He also prepared texts for the broadcast.

Soon messages of support began to reach the radio station, including those from overseas. Inevitably, too, however, the broadcasts came to the attention of the authorities.

Fearless Stance Towards Captors

President Ikeda
The youth took the precaution of doing their sound recordings and broadcasting in two different locations [to avoid being discovered by the authorities]. The greatest care was taken to ensure that the base for the radio broadcasts would not be located by the radio wave detector vehicles, operated by the police.

However, it was eventually discovered. The engineer who had helped them set up the radio station betrayed them by supplying information to the police. This type of person can be found anywhere.

The youth were to a certain extent prepared for the raid by the police. On that day, those who were usually responsible for the broadcast were reluctant to come in. Nevertheless, the broadcast had to go ahead. Dr Mehta and two others did the broadcast by themselves. They had even decided on a prearranged signal by which to enter and exit the room.

However, the police finally appeared, surrounding the youth's transmission base with a force of over a hundred.

At the time of the raid, the broadcast's closing song, 'Vande Mataram' — a song extolling the land of India — was playing. "What are you doing?' the police demanded.

Without missing a beat, Dr Mehta replied: "This is our national song. It would be courteous of you to stand up straight and listen to it!"

The police forgot all about arresting the young people and in spite of themselves, stood up straight, showing respect for the national song.

Dr Mehta has remarked that even now she does not know where these words came from. At a crucial moment, women are strong; they are calm and resolved.

The true Soka Gakkai spirit, too, is to rebut what is said to us tenfold or a hundredfold; it is to thoroughly reject unjust pressure, refute criticisms, and cry out for justice. The Soka Gakkai spirit is to be found in having the courage to fear absolutely nothing.

Courage that arises from a burning sense of justice is also the lifeblood of the battle for human rights.

Gandhi sought to teach the people of India this spirit of fearing nothing, to awaken them to their pride and dignity as a human being.

A Veritable Hell in Prison

Youth Representative
So, Dr Mehta was arrested.

President Ikeda
The two men who were with her were subjected to cruel torture, even electric shocks apparently. Dr Mehta was not tortured physically, but the inhumane interrogations she was put through amounted to spiritual torture. She has remarked of that time that her solitary prison cell was a veritable hell.

Outside, there were rumours that Dr Mehta had been receiving the same torture as the men, and many speculated that she would probably confess to the police and be let out of prison. Her mother, wishing to see her, went to the police station many times, but permission was not forthcoming. Finally, she was allowed to pass on some food for her daughter. In the container which held the food, Dr Mehta found a small piece of paper — a message from her mother. It said, "Should you be tortured and give in to the police, the doors of your home will not open to you even if you get out of prison."

Never give up; if you yield and get out of prison, you cannot come home — what a stout-hearted mother!

Dr Mehta says, "I was empowered by my mother's words. My mother was a woman with no education, but her powerful support was, more than anything, a great source of strength to me."

A Life Based on Faith

President Ikeda

Because of the military authorities' persecution of the Soka Gakkai during World War II, many top leaders in the organisation forsook their faith. This was in large part due to the weakness of their spouses' faith, who complained about their worries and fears. As a result, the determination of those leaders weakened, causing them to abandon their faith.

The faith of the person who is your partner in life exerts a decisive influence on you. No matter what trying circumstances you may find yourself in, you should never be cowardly. If you are, you will only align yourself with devilish functions.

On the other hand, no matter how high a position your partner might reach, you should never be deluded that this makes you in some way special or superior by mere association.

The important thing is that you be able to help wisely guide your partner, so that both of you may splendidly carry out your respective missions.

No matter what happens, good or bad, be true to yourself and live for *kosen-rufu*.

Truly respectworthy are those who proceed with the awareness: "Because of the SGI, I have learnt about the Mystic

Law and become happy, so it is only natural that I exert myself for the SGI and make efforts for *kosen-rufu*."

Eternal happiness belongs to such people.

Dr Mehta was sentenced to four years in prison. During that time, she had to endure cruel abuse, including having cement mixed into her meals, which damaged her health. However, she made it through her four-year sentence without being discouraged or defeated. It was a truly indomitable and tenacious battle.

"As Long As a Single Suffering Person Remains, I Will Fight"

Gandhi once remarked that though a prison cell may be a prison cell to a thief or burglar, to him it was a palace. He asserted that the true road to happiness was to be found in going to prison for the sake of one's country, the sake of one's religious convictions, and enduring the hardship and loss of liberty it entailed. Freedom, the Indian spiritual leader declared, could only be sought behind prison walls, or sometimes on the execution block. He maintained that it is not something one seeks in conference rooms, in the courts, or in the classroom. Gandhi's words are the words of a person who has built a palace within his own heart.

Mahatma Gandhi in jail: Gandhi insisted on being treated as an ordinary prisoner during the time he spent in the British prisons. The metal water container and plate were issued to all prisoners in Yerevda Jail.

Youth Representative

Far from weakening the resolve of Dr Usha Méhta (current president of the Gandhi Memorial Hall in Bombay), imprisonment forged and strengthened it.

President Ikeda

Gandhi also regarded imprisonment [for the sake of one's cause] as an honour. Whenever he heard that a friend or comrade had been imprisoned, he is said to have sent a congratulatory telegram.

Gandhi also once remarked that though a prison cell may be a prison cell to a thief or burglar, to him it was a palace. He asserted that the true road to happiness was to be found in going to prison for the sake of one's country, the sake of one's religious convictions, and enduring the hardship and loss of liberty it entailed. Freedom, the Indian spiritual leader declared, could only be sought behind prison walls, or sometimes on the execution block. He maintained that it is not something one seeks in conference rooms, in the courts, or in the classroom.

Gandhi's words are the words of a person who has built a palace within his own heart.

In total, Gandhi spent approximately six years and five months of his life in prison.

Gandhi was imprisoned for a total of 2,089 days in Indian prisons and 249 days in South African prisons.

A Change in Outlook

President Ikeda

This July (1993) marks the 50th anniversary of the imprisonment of the Soka Gakkai 1st and 2nd presidents, Tsunesaburo Makiguchi and Josei Toda (in 1943).

From prison, Mr Makiguchi wrote, "With a simple change of outlook, one can find enjoyment even in prison." But this sentence was censored.

In another letter, he also wrote, "Simply by changing your outlook, you can find safety even in hell." The word 'hell', as expected, was excised.

No doubt, the censors were offended that Mr Makiguchi

dared to describe the nation's prisons as 'hell', but their outlook was petty and small-minded compared to Mr Makiguchi's state of mind. At this stage, the prosecutors were still confident and swaggering. The world at large also, no doubt, believed that the prosecutors were far more important than their prisoner.

Without a firm philosophical basis, you cannot see a person's true greatness. Moreover, it is only when you yourself have gone through extraordinary hardship and suffering then only can you truly appreciate others' greatness.

We must never forget that it was because of Mr Toda that Mr Makiguchi's truth came to be known to the people. Mr Makiguchi was very fortunate to have a disciple, such as Mr Toda.

Out with the Usurpers!

President Ikeda

Just about the time Mr Makiguchi and Mr Toda were arrested, the slogan 'Quit India' was appearing throughout India.

"Imperialist rulers, immediately cease your illegal occupation of our land!" — this was the cry of the Indian people.

On August 8, 1942, the Working Committee of the All-India National Congress issued a statement demanding the immediate departure of the British. Shortly thereafter, Jawaharlal Nehru (1889-1964) [who was to become the first prime minister of independent India], Mahatma Gandhi, and the other leaders of the Indian independence movement were arrested by the British authorities.

Dr Mehta recalls, "When we adopted the 'Quit India' resolution, Gandhi and the rest of us did not think it was enough to simply achieve democracy and freedom for India alone. We were determined to keep up our struggle as long as people anywhere in the world were oppressed or experienced suffering, and that is what we have done."

Dr Mehta made these remarks on the occasion of the visit of the SGI 3rd youth division cultural exchange delegation to the Gandhi Memorial Hall in Bombay (on August 15, 1992).

She continued, "The fact that today, exactly fifty years later, I am able to welcome friends from Japan [who are also fighting for the suffering and oppressed] is, I believe, a result of our long struggle. I feel as if the spirit of the 'Quit India' campaign, which we struggled faithfully to defend, remains alive today, and I am filled with joy."

Ridding the World of Suffering

Youth Representative

Dr Mehta was overjoyed to feel this same spirit of fighting for suffering people pulsing in the youth of the SGI.

Dr Mehta remarked to the visiting SGI youth delegation, "President Ikeda expounds the teachings of Gandhi and works for the sake of peace. I offer my sincerest praise to President Ikeda and the SGI movement. Let us join forces and do our utmost to realise peace. I give my wholehearted support to the activities being promoted by President Ikeda."

President Ikeda

Mr Toda often said that he wanted to rid the world of the word 'suffering'. That was the truth that rested in the deepest depths of his heart.

There were those who saw Mr Toda superficially, who did not understand him, and who criticised him. But I knew what he was really like. That is why I came to the conclusion that to support and serve him was to serve the people of the world.

Seeking an End to War

President Ikeda

Dr Mehta has the warmest thoughts for the Japanese people, and particularly for the victims of the atomic bomb.

She said, "The Japanese people were baptised by the atomic bomb. Ever since that time, we at the Gandhi Memorial Hall in Bombay have organised marches on August 6 and August 9 each year to remember the victims and call for an end to war … I believe that the arrival of our young friends from Japan today (August 15, the day India gained independence in 1947) marks one of the fruits of our activities."

The strength of Dr Mehta's emotion is palpable.

August 15 is India's Independence Day. Usha Gokani, Gandhi's granddaughter, also met our youth division members on this day. I am deeply grateful for the kindness of both Dr

Mehta and Dr Gokani, who took the time to meet our members on such an important and busy day.

Sakyamuni is the Source of the Philosophy of Non-violence

The *Saddharma-Pundarika-Sutra*—The Lotus Sutra read by Gandhi. (Published in 1908)

President Ikeda

Dr Mehta once remarked, "Gandhi's philosophy of non-violence can be traced back to Sakyamuni. Non-violence is not simply an absence of violence. It is a positive spirit of compassion and love for all living things, and action based on that spirit … Like Sakyamuni, Gandhi had compassion for those who were suffering. And, his compassion did not stop with human beings. He was saddened by harm done to animals and plants, to any living thing."

This brings to mind a certain episode in which a family of untouchables visited Gandhi's ashram.

The untouchables are a much discriminated group of people in Indian society, so low in status that they are even below and outside the caste system.

The couple and their young daughter wished to live with

Gandhi lived in the Sewagram Ashram from 1936 to 1946, which was an important centre for the freedom movement of India. The *ashram* is built of mud, mud-bricks, bamboo, lime and clay-tiles. Gandhi planted trees around the *ashram* and encouraged the inmates to do the same.

Gandhi in the ashram, and he permitted it. The other members of the ashram fell into a panic. It wasn't just that discrimination against the untouchable class persisted. The wealthy sponsors of the ashram refused to continue to support an 'unclean place', placing the ashram in financial peril.

Gandhi responded with an unruffled calm, "If we can no longer keep the ashram running, let us all move to the village of untouchables and live there."

The ashram was able to overcome its financial difficulties due to the support of an anonymous sponsor, but it was difficult indeed to change the attitudes of the others living in this small community.

Gandhi adopted the couple's child as his own and continued to protect the family.

Gandhi always said that he did not wish to be born again, but in the case that he was reborn, he hoped it would be as an untouchable, so that he might understand and share their sadness and suffering, and the insult and scorn they must bear. It was his wish to save them from that tragic state.

Gandhi called the untouchables the *Harijans*, the children of God.

Nichiren Daishonin was Discriminated Against

Youth Representative
The fight against discrimination is the very core of the fight for human rights.

President Ikeda
Recently, I proposed publishing a dialogue with Austregésilo de Athayde, the former president of the Brazilian Academy of Letters, tentatively, titled *Human Rights in the 21st Century*. Dr Athayde's immediate and emphatic response to this proposal was: "In the discussion of human rights, I am certain that the struggle against discrimination will be the central issue. All human beings are equal. No discrimination is permissible. It is absolutely unacceptable."

It is important to put yourself in the shoes of those who are discriminated against.

Gandhi always said that he did not wish to be born again but in the case that he was reborn, he hoped it would be as an untouchable, so that he might understand and share their sadness and suffering, and the insult and scorn they must bear.

Nichiren Daishonin said of himself on more than one occasion: "I, Nichiren is the son of a *chandala*[1] family," (*WND*, pg 202) and "Nichiren, who in this life was born poor and

---

[1]. *Chandala*: In ancient India, a class of people who worked at handling corpses, butchering animals, or other professions bound to the death of living creatures. Despised as untouchable, they ranked below the lowest of the four classes within the Brahmanic social order. Because the Daishonin was the child of a fisherman, he refers to himself as 'the son of a *chandala* family'.

lowly to a *chandala* family." (*WND*, pg 303)

Both of these statements are contained in the Gosho written by the Daishonin during his exile on Sado Island. Here, he draws attention to the true greatness of the unadorned human being, in contrast to the highly discriminatory behaviour so often displayed by those in positions of power and authority.

"Though I may seem poor and lowly, my heart and mind is that of a king," — we may read in this spirit the Daishonin's invincible declaration of humanity and human rights.

For Nichiren Daishonin, the act of discarding his transient status and revealing his true identity as the original Buddha did not mean placing himself on a pedestal, out of reach of ordinary people. Quite the opposite. The Daishonin regarded himself as equal to the most oppressed, the most deeply suffering, the lowliest of all.

We must give serious thought to the Daishonin's conduct and behaviour, and to his struggle for human rights.

Youth Representative

In this respect alone, it is clear that the blatant discrimination shown by the priests of the Nikken sect flagrantly contradicts the intentions of Nichiren Daishonin. The enemies of human rights are the enemies of Buddhism and the enemies of humankind.

President Ikeda

One hundred years ago (in June 1893), Gandhi, who had just arrived in South Africa, was expelled from a passenger train simply because of the colour of his skin. Though he possessed a first-class ticket, only white people were allowed to ride first class.

If Gandhi had reacted to this so-called 'Pieter-maritzburg Station Incident' by simply turning the other cheek, there might have been no battle for civil rights in South Africa, and the history of India's struggle for independence would have been very different as well.

[In the face of injustice,] we must not be silent; we must rise up.

Gandhi's struggle was to become a starting point for the great movement against apartheid in South Africa. Through Martin Luther King Jr, (1929-1968), Gandhi also exerted a decisive influence on the American civil rights movement.

The courageous cry of a single individual standing up for justice lights a torch in the hearts of thousands and changes the course of human history.

Establishing a Society Free of Violence and Discrimination

President Ikeda

Gandhi also fought to improve the social position of women. This, too, is an essential part of the human rights struggle.

Dr Mehta said, "Gandhi taught us this: 'Fight courageously for what is right. Speak the truth,' and 'By gaining peace for the hearts of women, you will establish a peaceful society. At that

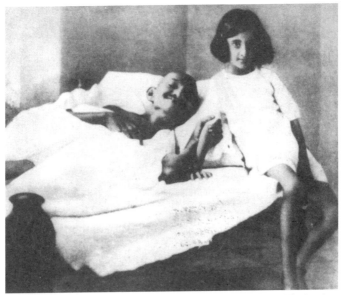

Gandhi with the then six years old Indira Nehru (later Indira Gandhi), daughter of Jawaharlal Nehru. (Delhi, September 1924).

time, the peaceful power of women will become a great and explosive force that will change society.'"

I have heard it said that just before India's independence was declared, there was a heated discussion about who should be the first president. Gandhi apparently commented that he would like to see a young girl, as pure as crystal and possessing a tenacious spirit, as the first president of India. He added that he would select her from among the untouchable class.

Gandhi was pointing out that though independence had been achieved, discrimination still existed, as did rivalry and

46

violence between religions. He undoubtedly hoped to change India into a humanitarian state, free of violence or discrimination. He did not even attend the independence ceremonies.

Gandhi's declaration that he would choose an untouchable girl for president is alive with his fervent prayers [for the peace and happiness of his country] and his great faith in women. I also feel that it resounds with a cry from the heart: "The fight has only just begun!"

First Edition, 2003
Reprinted 2004, 2005

Copyright Soka Gakkai © 2003

Gandhi—A Discussion on the Struggle for Human Rights
by Daisaku Ikeda

Published by Soka Gakkai Malaysia (SGM)
Wisma Kebudayaan SGM
243 Jalan Bukit Bintang, 55100 Kuala Lumpur, Malaysia
Tel: 603-2141 2003

Translation: The SGI Newsletter

Art Design: Chew Meng Tatt

Printed in Malaysia by Gainwell Enterprise